X-Matrix

| Correlation | | Correlation/Contribution | Accountability |

Tactics

Strategies

X

Targets

Results

| Correlation | | Correlation/ Contribution | |

Team Members

Revenue
Development Costs
Material Costs
Conversion Costs
Value Stream Profit

● Strong correlation

○ Moderate Correlation

△ Weak Correlation

X-Matrix

Correlation

Correlation/Contribution

Accountability

Team Members

Tactics

Strategies

X

Targets

Results

Revenue
Development Costs
Material Costs
Conversion Costs
Value Stream Profit

Correlation

Correlation/ Contribution

● Strong correlation

○ Moderate Correlation

△ Weak Correlation

www.enna.com

X-Matrix

Correlation		Correlation/Contribution		Accountability

Tactics

Strategies

X

Targets

Results

Team Members

	Revenue
	Development Costs
	Material Costs
	Conversion Costs
	Value Stream Profit

Correlation

Correlation/ Contribution

● Strong correlation

○ Moderate Correlation

△ Weak Correlation

X-Matrix

Correlation		Correlation/Contribution		Accountability

Tactics

Strategies

X

Targets

Results

Revenue	
Development Costs	
Material Costs	
Conversion Costs	
Value Stream Profit	

Team Members

Correlation	Correlation/ Contribution

● Strong correlation

○ Moderate Correlation

△ Weak Correlation

X-Matrix

| Correlation | | Correlation/Contribution | Accountability |

Tactics

Strategies

X

Targets

Results

Revenue
Development Costs
Material Costs
Conversion Costs
Value Stream Profit

Team Members

| Correlation | | Correlation/ Contribution | |

● Strong correlation

○ Moderate Correlation

△ Weak Correlation

www.enna.com

X-Matrix

Correlation	Tactics	Correlation/Contribution	Accountability

Team Members

Strategies

X

Targets

Results

| Revenue |
| Development Costs |
| Material Costs |
| Conversion Costs |
| Value Stream Profit |

Correlation	Correlation/ Contribution

● Strong correlation

○ Moderate Correlation

△ Weak Correlation

X-Matrix

Correlation/Contribution

Accountability

Team Members

Tactics

Strategies

X

Targets

Results

	Revenue	
	Development Costs	
	Material Costs	
	Conversion Costs	
	Value Stream Profit	

Correlation

Correlation/ Contribution

● Strong correlation

○ Moderate Correlation

△ Weak Correlation

www.enna.com

X-Matrix

Correlation		Correlation/Contribution	Accountability

Tactics

Strategies

X

Targets

Results

Team Members

Revenue
Development Costs
Material Costs
Conversion Costs
Value Stream Profit

Correlation		Correlation/ Contribution

● Strong correlation

○ Moderate Correlation

△ Weak Correlation

www.enna.com

X-Matrix

X-Matrix

Correlation

Correlation/Contribution

Accountability

Team Members

Tactics

Strategies

X

Targets

Results

Revenue

Development Costs

Material Costs

Conversion Costs

Value Stream Profit

Correlation

Correlation/ Contribution

● Strong correlation

○ Moderate Correlation

△ Weak Correlation

© ENNA
KNOWLEDGE INTO PRACTICE

www.enna.com

X-Matrix

Correlation		Correlation/Contribution	Accountability

Tactics

Strategies **X** **Targets**

Results

Correlation	Revenue		Correlation/ Contribution
	Development Costs		
	Material Costs		
	Conversion Costs		
	Value Stream Profit		

Team Members

● Strong correlation

○ Moderate Correlation

△ Weak Correlation

© *ENNA®*
KNOWLEDGE INTO PRACTICE

www.enna.com

X-Matrix

Correlation		Correlation/Contribution		Accountability

Tactics

Strategies

X

Targets

Results

Team Members

Revenue
Development Costs
Material Costs
Conversion Costs
Value Stream Profit

Correlation		Correlation/ Contribution

● Strong correlation

○ Moderate Correlation

△ Weak Correlation

X-Matrix

Correlation		Correlation/Contribution		Accountability

Tactics

Strategies

X

Targets

Results

Team Members

Revenue
Development Costs
Material Costs
Conversion Costs
Value Stream Profit

Correlation		Correlation/ Contribution

● Strong correlation

○ Moderate Correlation

△ Weak Correlation

X-Matrix

Correlation		Correlation/Contribution	Accountability

Team Members

Tactics

Strategies **X** Targets

Results

Revenue
Development Costs
Material Costs
Conversion Costs
Value Stream Profit

Correlation		Correlation/ Contribution	

● Strong correlation

○ Moderate Correlation

△ Weak Correlation

www.enna.com

X-Matrix

Correlation		Correlation/Contribution	Accountability

Tactics

Strategies

X

Targets

Results

Revenue
Development Costs
Material Costs
Conversion Costs
Value Stream Profit

Team Members

Correlation		Correlation/ Contribution	

● Strong correlation

○ Moderate Correlation

△ Weak Correlation

X-Matrix

Correlation

Correlation/Contribution

Accountability

Team Members

Tactics

Strategies

X

Targets

Results

Revenue
Development Costs
Material Costs
Conversion Costs
Value Stream Profit

Correlation

Correlation/ Contribution

● Strong correlation

○ Moderate Correlation

△ Weak Correlation

X-Matrix

Correlation		Correlation/Contribution	Accountability

Tactics

Strategies

X

Targets

Results

Team Members

Revenue	
Development Costs	
Material Costs	
Conversion Costs	
Value Stream Profit	

Correlation		Correlation/ Contribution

● Strong correlation

○ Moderate Correlation

△ Weak Correlation

Correlation		Correlation/Contribution		Accountability

Tactics

Strategies

X

Targets

Results

| Revenue |
| Development Costs |
| Material Costs |
| Conversion Costs |
| Value Stream Profit |

Team Members

Correlation/ Contribution

● Strong correlation

○ Moderate Correlation

△ Weak Correlation

X-Matrix

Correlation

Correlation/Contribution

Accountability

Team Members

Tactics

Strategies

X

Targets

Results

Revenue

Development Costs

Material Costs

Conversion Costs

Value Stream Profit

Correlation

Correlation/ Contribution

● Strong correlation

○ Moderate Correlation

△ Weak Correlation

X-Matrix

Correlation	Tactics	Correlation/Contribution	Accountability

Tactics

Strategies X **Targets**

Results

| Revenue |
| Development Costs |
| Material Costs |
| Conversion Costs |
| Value Stream Profit |

| Correlation | | Correlation/ Contribution |

Team Members

● Strong correlation

○ Moderate Correlation

△ Weak Correlation

www.enna.com

X-Matrix

Correlation		Correlation/Contribution	Accountability

Tactics

X

Strategies

Targets

Results

	Revenue	
	Development Costs	
	Material Costs	
	Conversion Costs	
	Value Stream Profit	

Team Members

Correlation		Correlation/ Contribution

● Strong correlation

○ Moderate Correlation

△ Weak Correlation

www.enna.com

X-Matrix

Correlation/Contribution

Accountability

Team Members

Tactics

Strategies

X

Targets

Results

Revenue
Development Costs
Material Costs
Conversion Costs
Value Stream Profit

Correlation

Correlation/ Contribution

● Strong correlation

○ Moderate Correlation

△ Weak Correlation

X-Matrix

Correlation		Correlation/Contribution		Accountability

Tactics

X

Strategies

Targets

Results

	Revenue	
	Development Costs	
	Material Costs	
	Conversion Costs	
	Value Stream Profit	

Team Members

Correlation

Correlation/ Contribution

● Strong correlation

○ Moderate Correlation

△ Weak Correlation

© ENNA
KNOWLEDGE INTO PRACTICE

www.enna.com

X-Matrix

Correlation		Tactics		Correlation/Contribution		Accountability

Team Members

Strategies

X

Targets

Results

Revenue
Development Costs
Material Costs
Conversion Costs
Value Stream Profit

Correlation			Correlation/ Contribution

⬤ Strong correlation

◯ Moderate Correlation

△ Weak Correlation

X-Matrix

Correlation		Correlation/Contribution	Accountability

Tactics

Strategies

X

Targets

Results

Revenue
Development Costs
Material Costs
Conversion Costs
Value Stream Profit

Team Members

Correlation		Correlation/ Contribution	

● Strong correlation

○ Moderate Correlation

△ Weak Correlation

www.enna.com

X-Matrix

Correlation		Correlation/Contribution	Accountability

Tactics

Strategies

X

Targets

Results

Correlation		Correlation/ Contribution

Revenue

Development Costs

Material Costs

Conversion Costs

Value Stream Profit

Team Members

● Strong correlation

○ Moderate Correlation

△ Weak Correlation

www.enna.com